Introduction to
Natural Light Photographic Portraiture

Indoors and Out

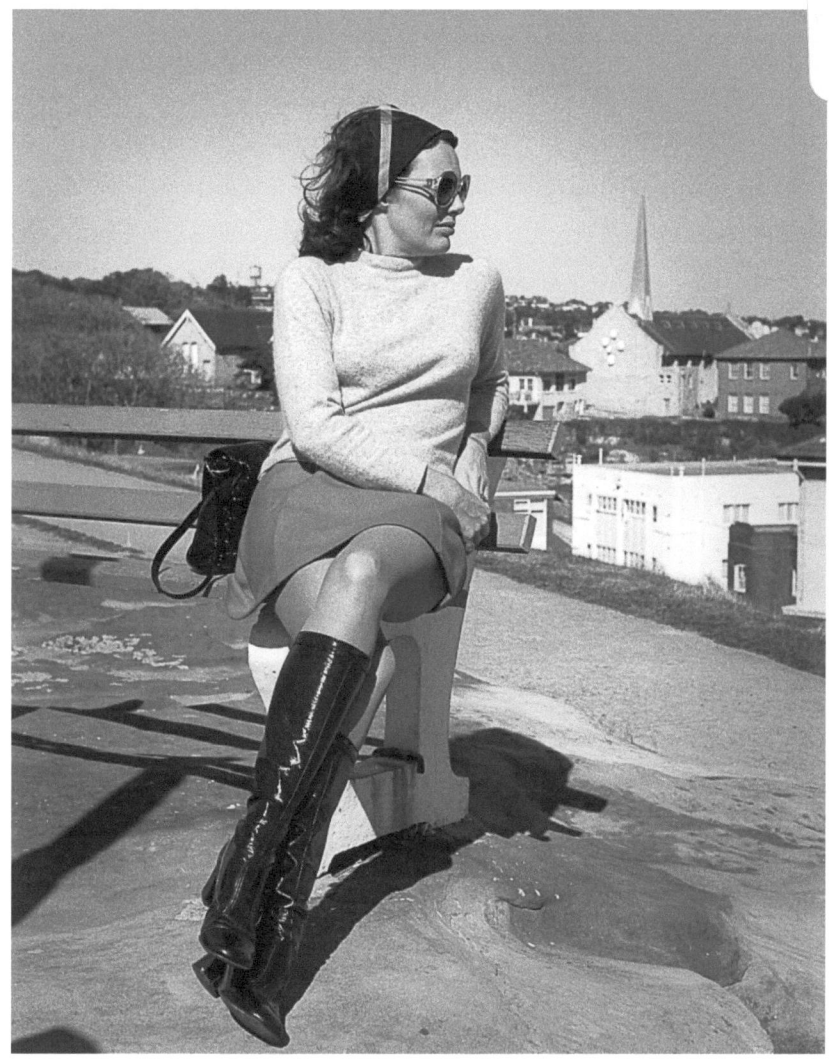

David Bigwood, LRPS

Published by David Bigwood publishing

Copyright 2018 David Bigwood

The material in this electronic publication is protected under International Copyright Laws and Treaties, and as such, any unauthorised reprint or use of this material is strictly prohibited.

The material in this electronic publication can be stored only on one computer at one time. You may not copy, forward, or transfer this publication or any part of it, whether in electronic or printed form, to another person or entity.

Reproduction or translation of any part of this work without the permission of the copyright holder is against the law.

About the Author

David Bigwood is a regularly published writer and photographer with his work having been used in well over sixty publications, mainly in Australia and the United Kingdom.

He started freelancing in the days of black and white film when he made pictures of his children which sold as 10x8 prints to several UK and Australian magazines.

He has qualified as a Licentiate of the Royal Photographic Society (LRPS) with a panel of black and white prints and is a former member of the Australian Society of Authors.

For three years he was a columnist on freelancing for the UK magazine *F2 Freelance and Digital*. He has written a number of articles for *Australian Photography*, *Australian Camera* and *Better Photography*.

He founded and edited *The Black and White Enthusiast* magazine (later *Silvershotz*) and was sometime editor of the *Journal of the Australian Photographic Society*.

He sells images to publications through Alamy, the on-line photography library.

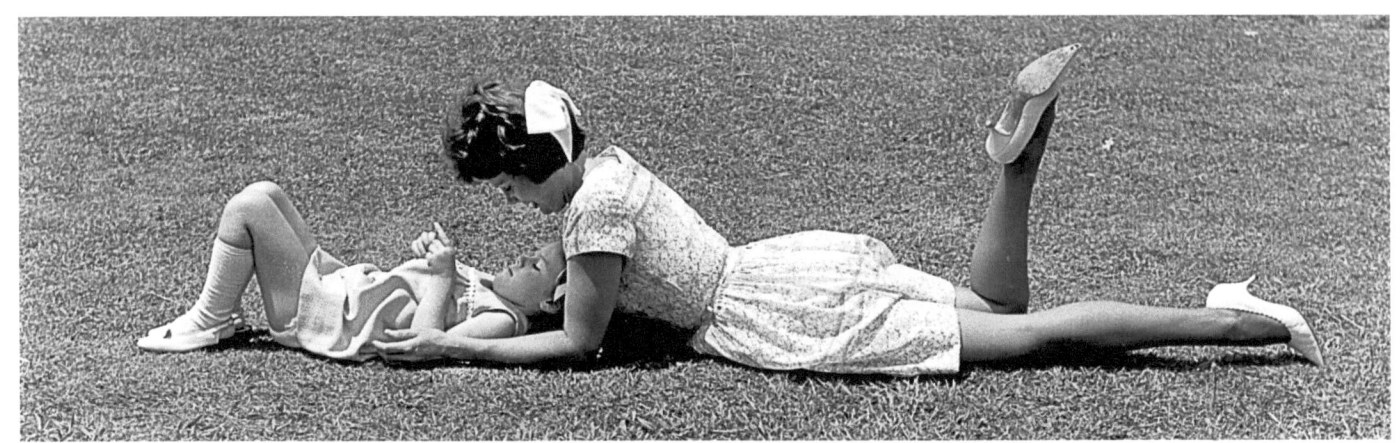
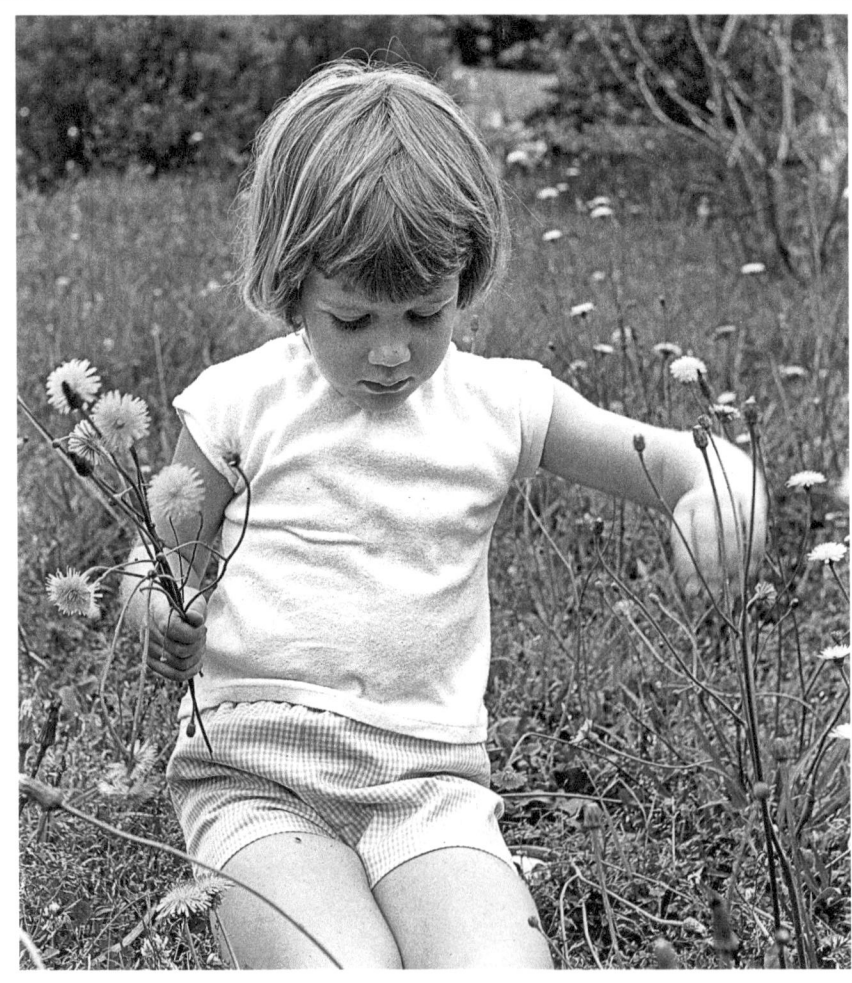

Introduction

Making pictures of people had been the province of artists with pencil and paint before photography came along. Portraiture then added another medium to its bow as photographers made its genre popular from the start. We have all seen some of the early results from the comparatively clumsy cameras of the Victorians. We may consider the pictures stiff and excessively formal but at least we have an inkling of how that era was.

Today, making pictures of people is probably the number one subject for camera and mobile phones. Sadly most of these pictures may never see the light of day ending up on a computer or languishing on a phone until a computer crash or a phone malfunction sends them off to the ether never to be seen again.

The aim of this e-book is to encourage you to make such worthwhile pictures of your friends and family that you will want to preserve the results as prints which will show the people of fifty or a hundred years time what we were like in the beginning of the twenty-first century.

I have chosen to show pictures that have been made by natural light, both indoors and out, as I think this light produces some of the best illumination you can use to get natural portraits as many professional portrait photographers know. And, if it is good enough for them, it's good enough for me.

If you have any questions, you can e-mail them to me through davidbigwoodpublishing.blog/contact/ and I will do my best to answer them.

Daylight Indoors

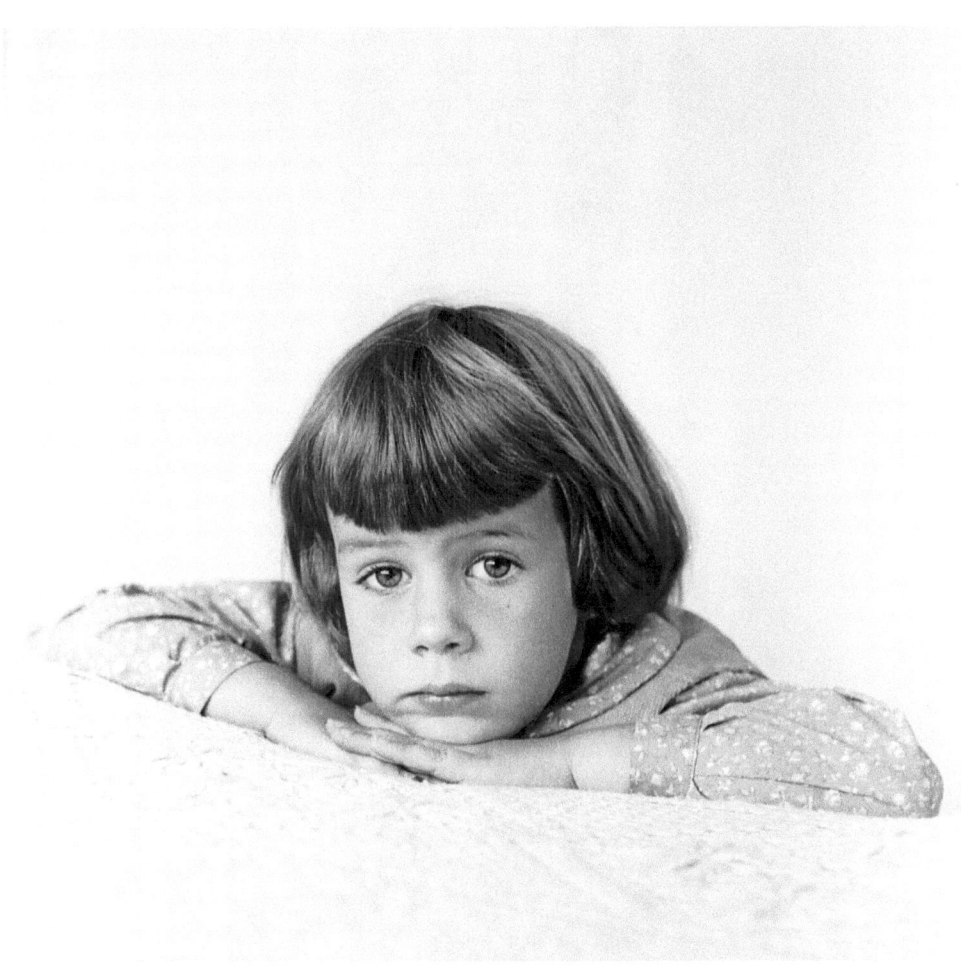

This picture of my daughter was a casual portrait as she leant on our bed one morning. I can't remember what it was that she wanted but I was so taken by the naturalness of the pose that I grabbed my camera and captured it.

The soft light was from the windows on the other side of the room with some reflection from the light bedspread she was leaning on. You can see the catch-light from the window in her eyes.

It is one of my favourite pictures of her as a little girl and it would have been almost impossible to duplicate the expression in a studio lit shot.

Another morning in our bedroom. It was becoming quite a studio! I love the soft light provided through the windows which has captured her hair beautifully. This picture has been used in a UK magazine to illustrate an article on sick children. I hasten to add, she was perfectly healthy when this picture was made.

Once again it is the naturalness of the pose that makes the picture. The light was there, the pose was right and all I had to do was press the camera button. If I had had to use flash the atmosphere would have been lost. And studio lighting would have taken a lot of expertise to capture the softness of the natural light.

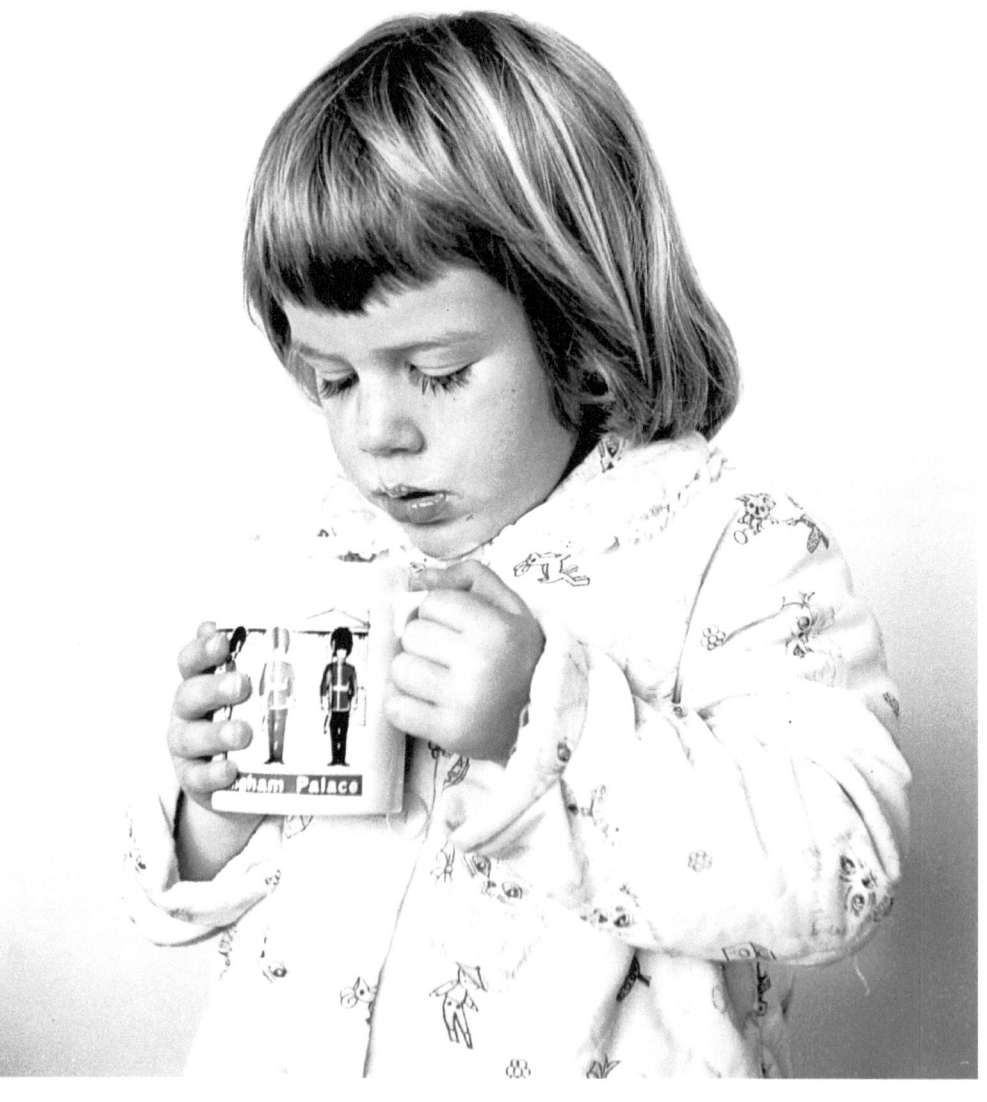

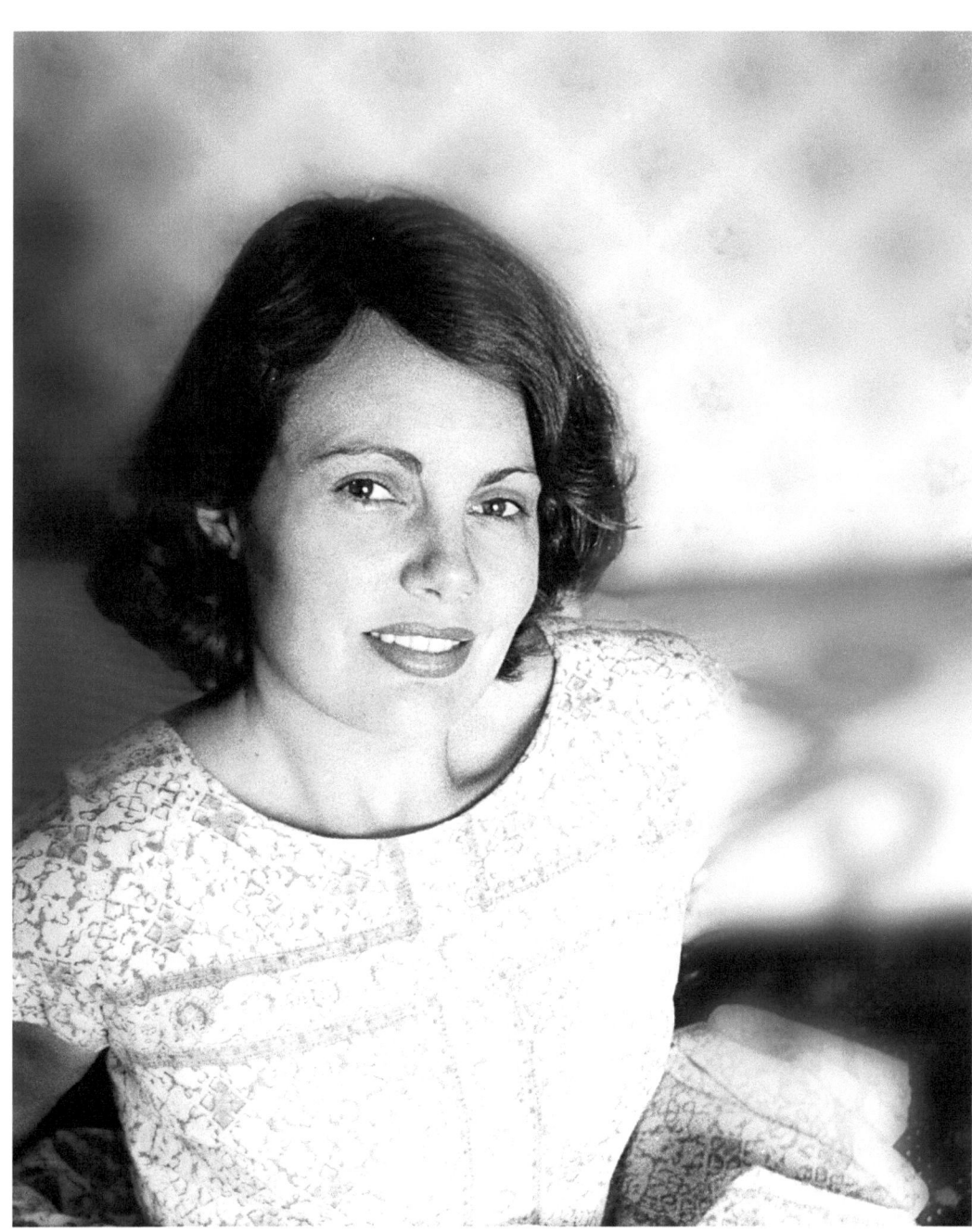

Another portrait softly lit from a window several feet away from the subject. You can see the catch-light from the window in her eyes.

In the original negative the eye was distracted from the sitter because the background wallpaper and cushion were too sharp (should have used a wider aperture!) but post processing in Photoshop has enabled me to blur the offending background and so reduce its effect.

One of the great benefits of using natural light is that the sitter does not have a feeling of being overpowered by studio lights glaring at her. This is especially true with non-professional models.

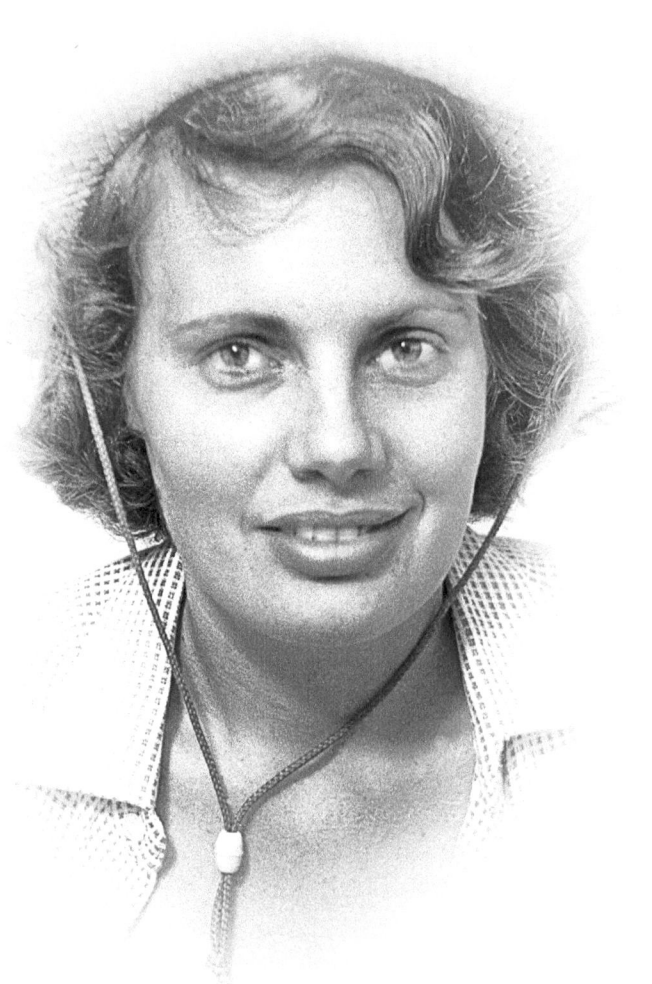

The softness of the light from the window directly opposite the sitter has made the picture suitable for the vignetting that I have applied in post processing. The window had venetian blinds which enabled me to have some control over the amount of light falling on the subject.

These blinds are just one of the controls I have when shooting with natural light. Others include a sheet of white cardboard to bounce some reflected light onto the shadow side of a face and the application of greaseproof paper to a window if the light is too bright.

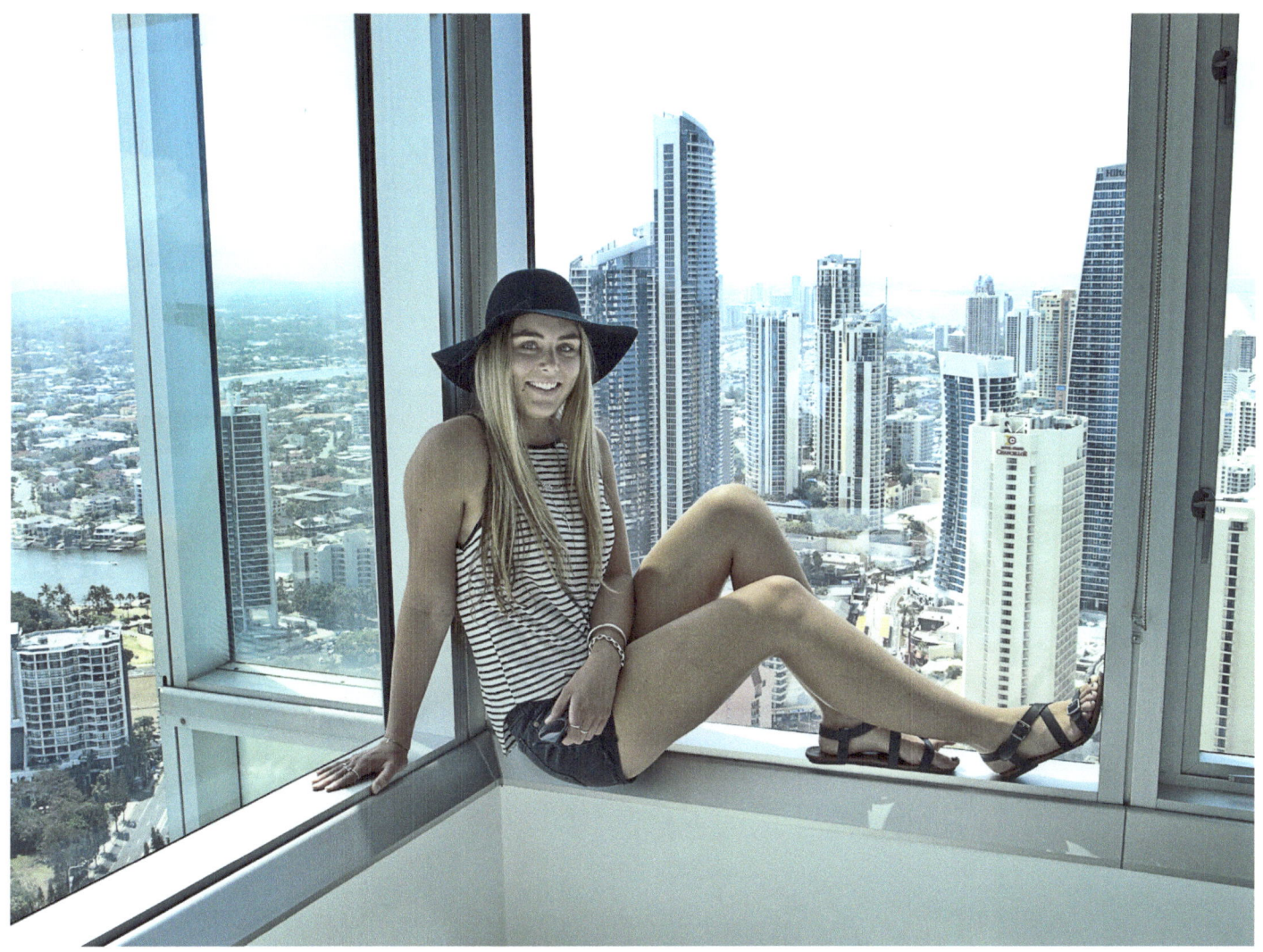

On this occasion the windows were so placed that I was able to include them in the picture while allowing the natural light to illuminate the model.

Under normal circumstances the light would have probably been too strong to enable the making of a suitable picture but on this day the overcast sky produced the soft light that works so well with portraiture.

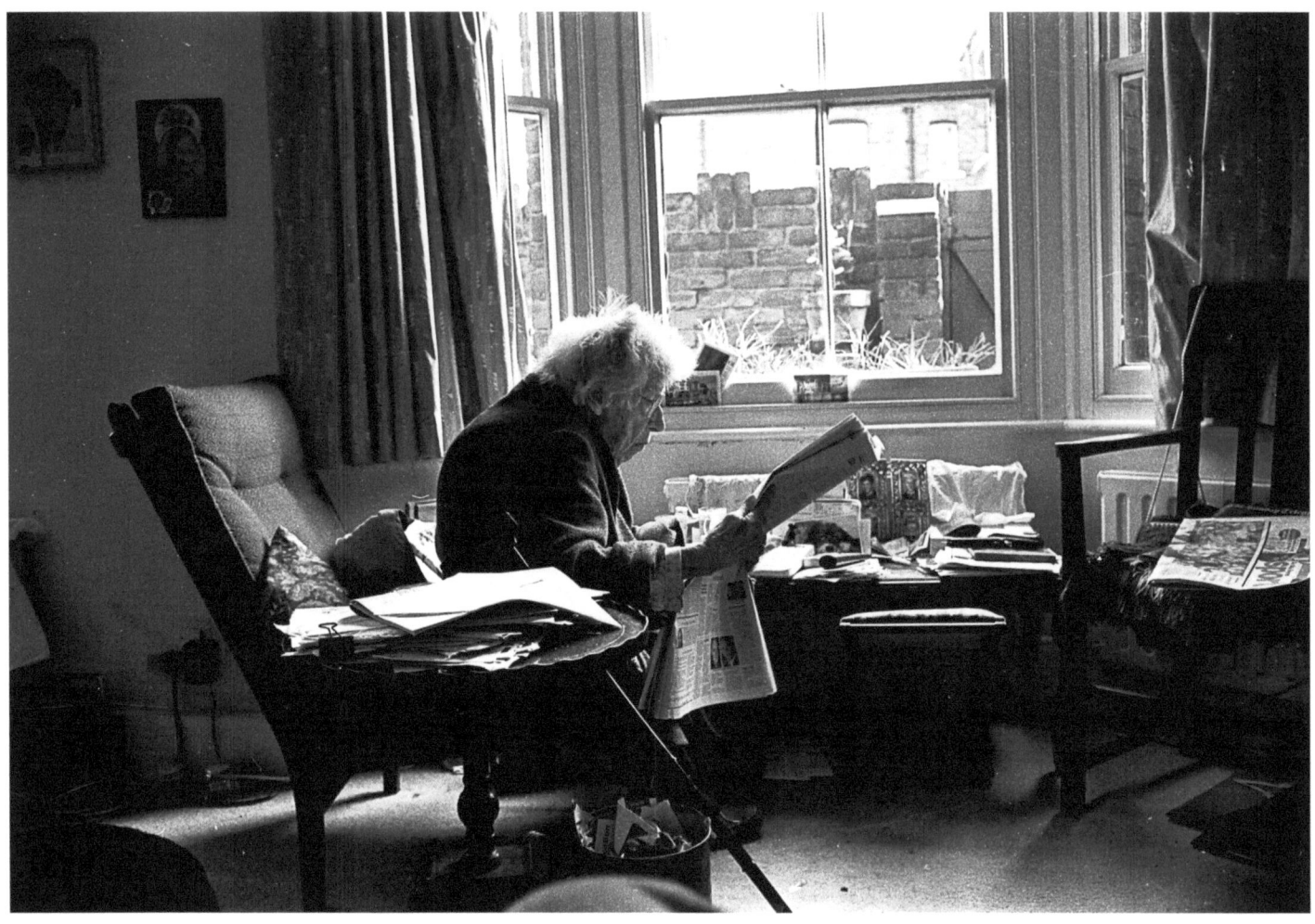

Portraiture need not be just a picture of an individual. Sometimes the story of that individual is better told by including something of their environment. In this case the old lady is surrounded by the things that help to make her life comfortable.

I think the contre jour treatment and the black and white picture tells the story well. The shot was made without disturbing her morning routine. No bright flash and certainly no studio lights — if I had even suggested that I was about to make a picture she would have been horrified! So, natural light to the rescue and a quietly made picture enables me to remember something of the last years of my mother's life.

Daylight Outdoors

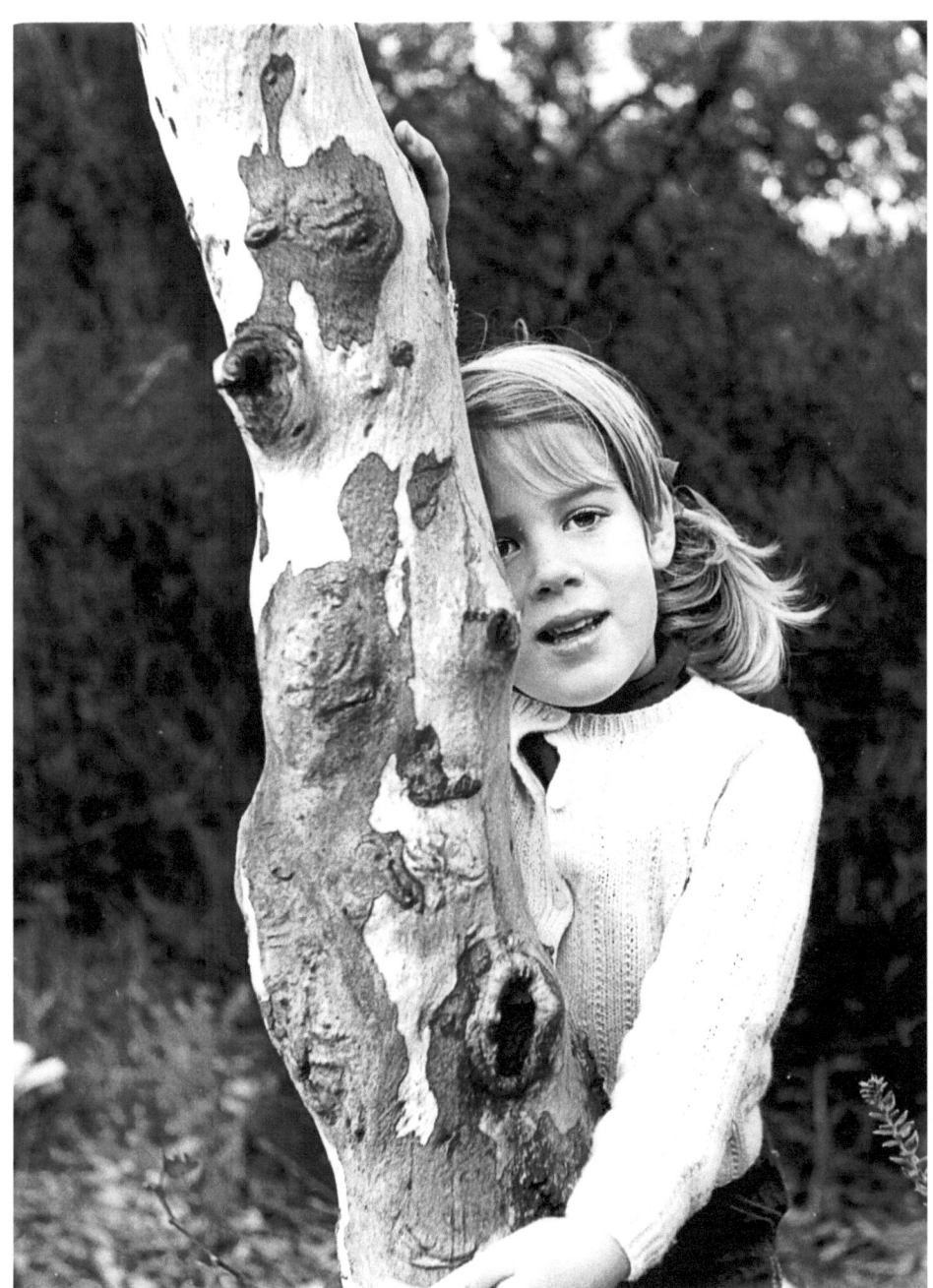

A lovely overcast day giving gentle soft light and my beautiful model ready to let Dad make some more pictures while she hugged a tree. What more could a father and photographer want!

If it is not such an overcast day then searching for suitable light shaded spots to make your pictures is the next best thing.

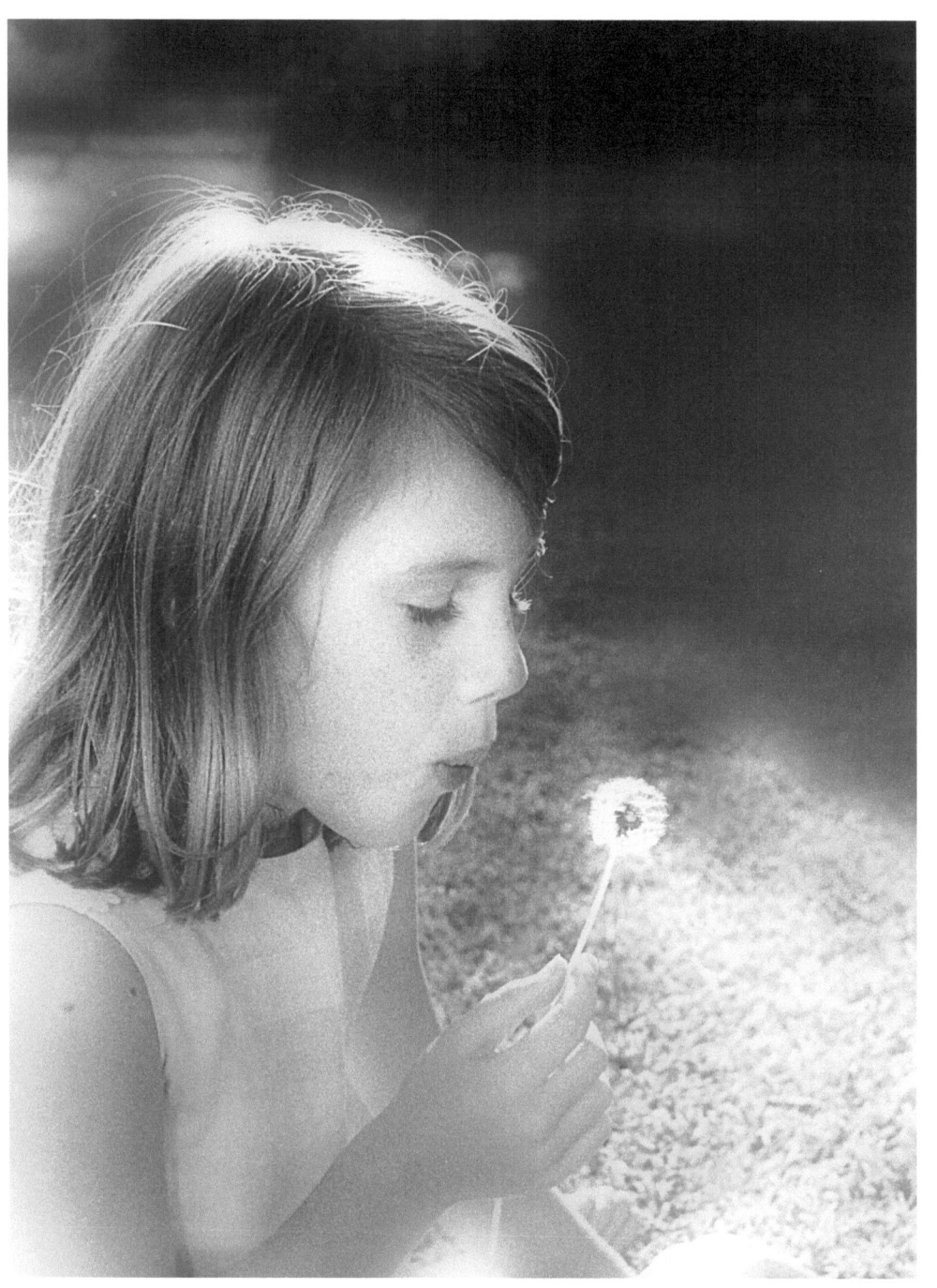

The light was much stronger for this shot so I managed to get my daughter facing away from the strong sunlight which then lit her hair from behind. I also processed the picture to blur the background and add a gentle glow.

If you are out in strong sunlight, try to pose your subject with their back to the sun. It's more comfortable for them and they will appreciate your picture without them squinting. Take a meter reading off their face and use a lens hood on your camera.

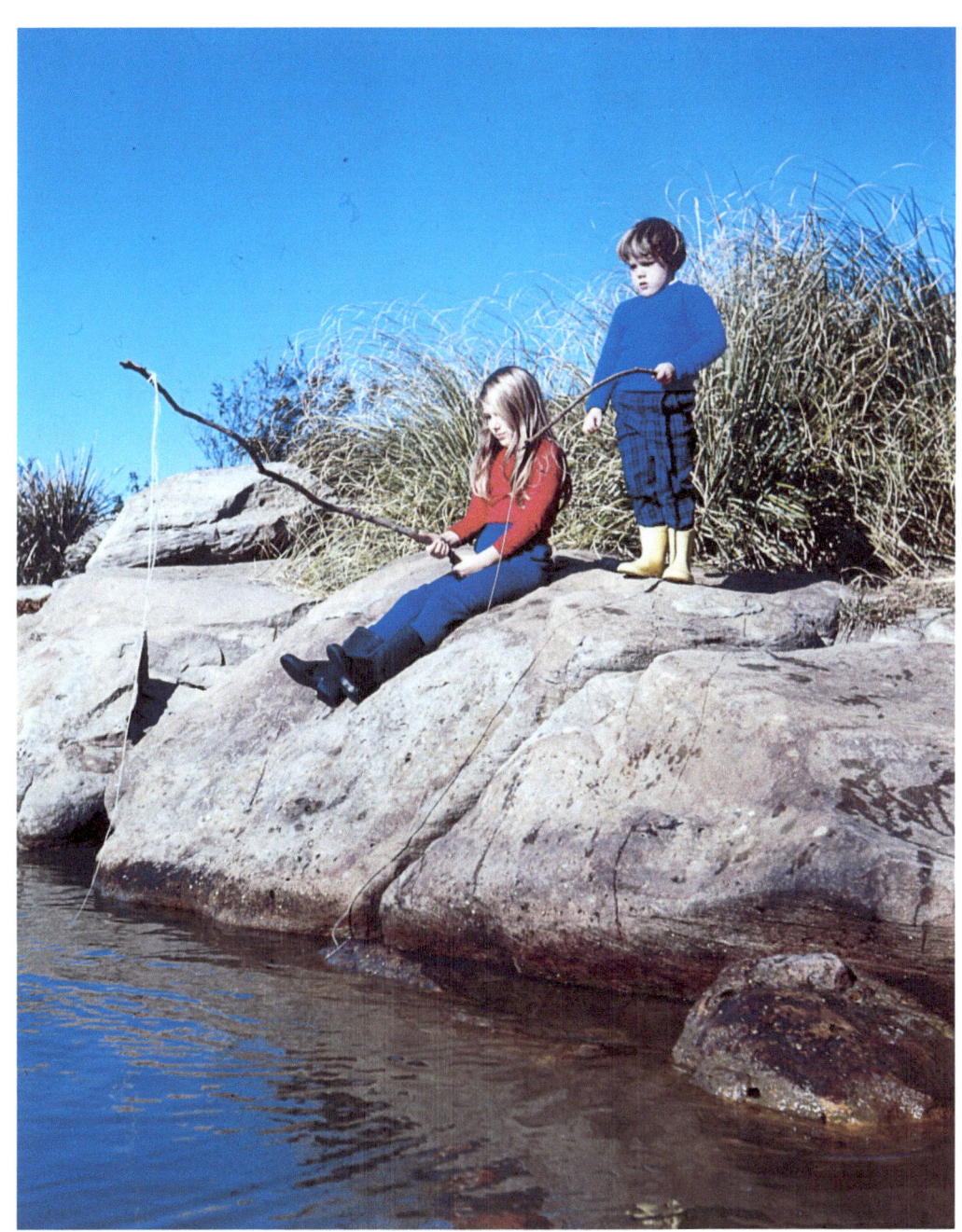

Even though the sun is shining directly on the faces of the subjects they are far enough away from the camera that any squinting is undetectable. It is a very childlike scene with them both 'concentrating' on their pretend fishing.

It was used in a book of encouraging sayings.

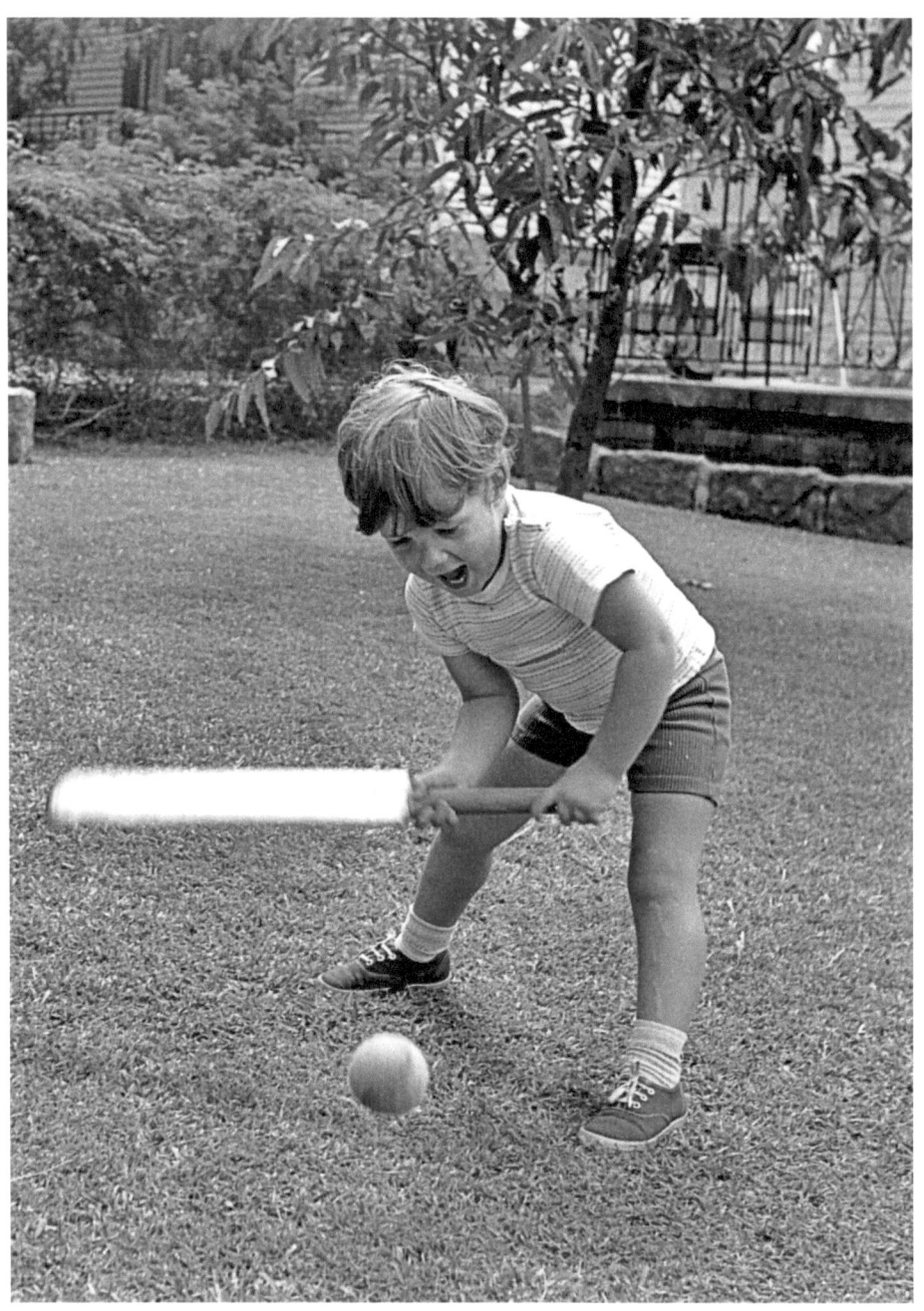

Is this a portrait? Some may consider it just a picture of a boy at play but I think it says a lot more than that. I see it as a healthy young boy who is happy that he has someone to toss him a ball that he can try to whack with his cricket bat. It's a lot more than just a boy at play.

Once again it was made under a lightly overcast sky so there were no harsh shadows.

And, yes he did go on to be a very good club cricketer.

Does a portrait have to show a face? Obviously this picture shows that I don't think it does. But, as far as you are concerned, it is your choice. It was the sparkling light on the water that caught my eye as my daughter sat on the rock pretend fishing. That and the highlights on her hair and on the unravelling sisal string on her 'fishing rod'. A good lens hood is essential for this type of photography. I took the meter reading off the non-sparkling part of the water which I knew would render my subject as a semi silhouette.

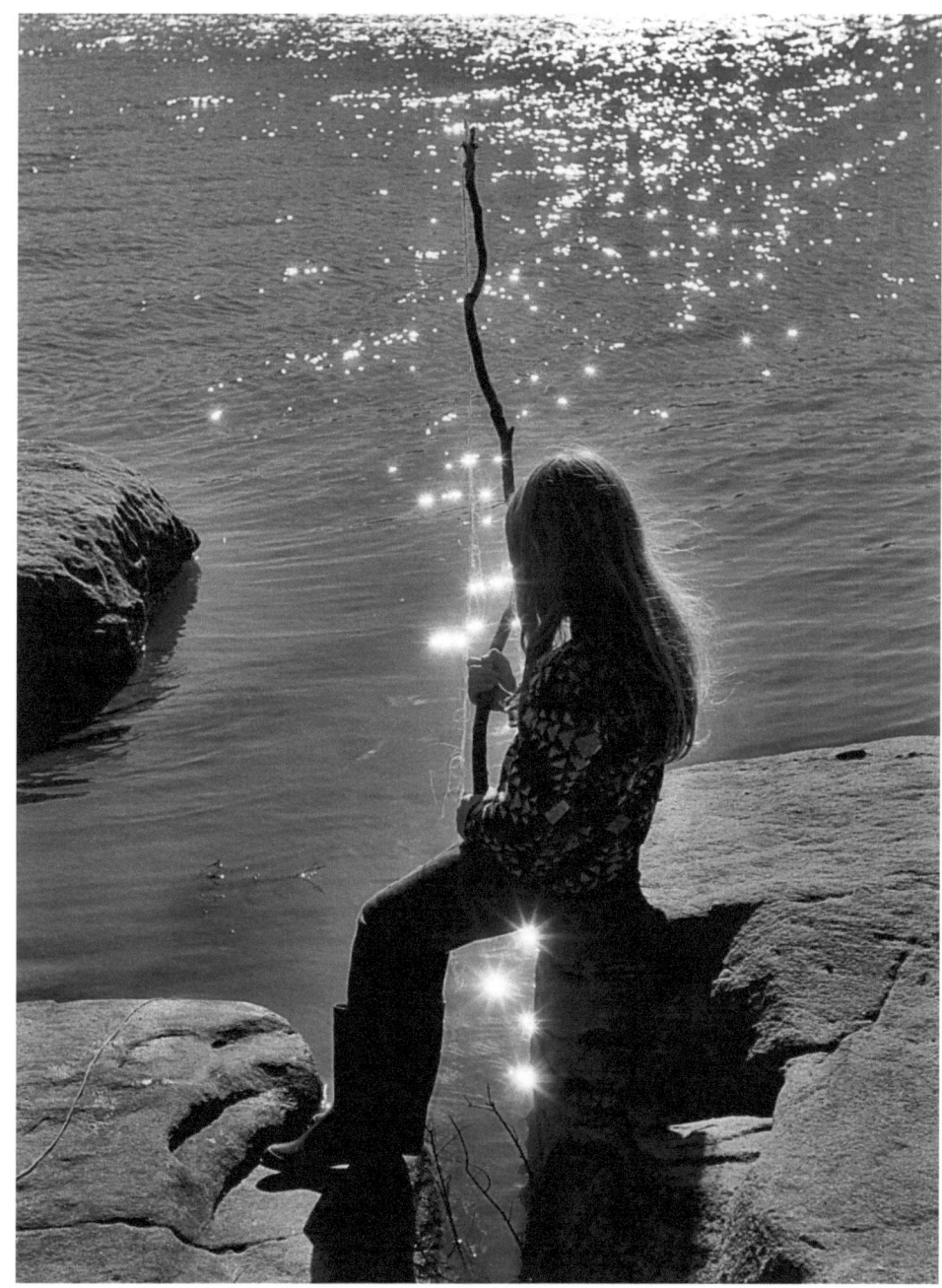

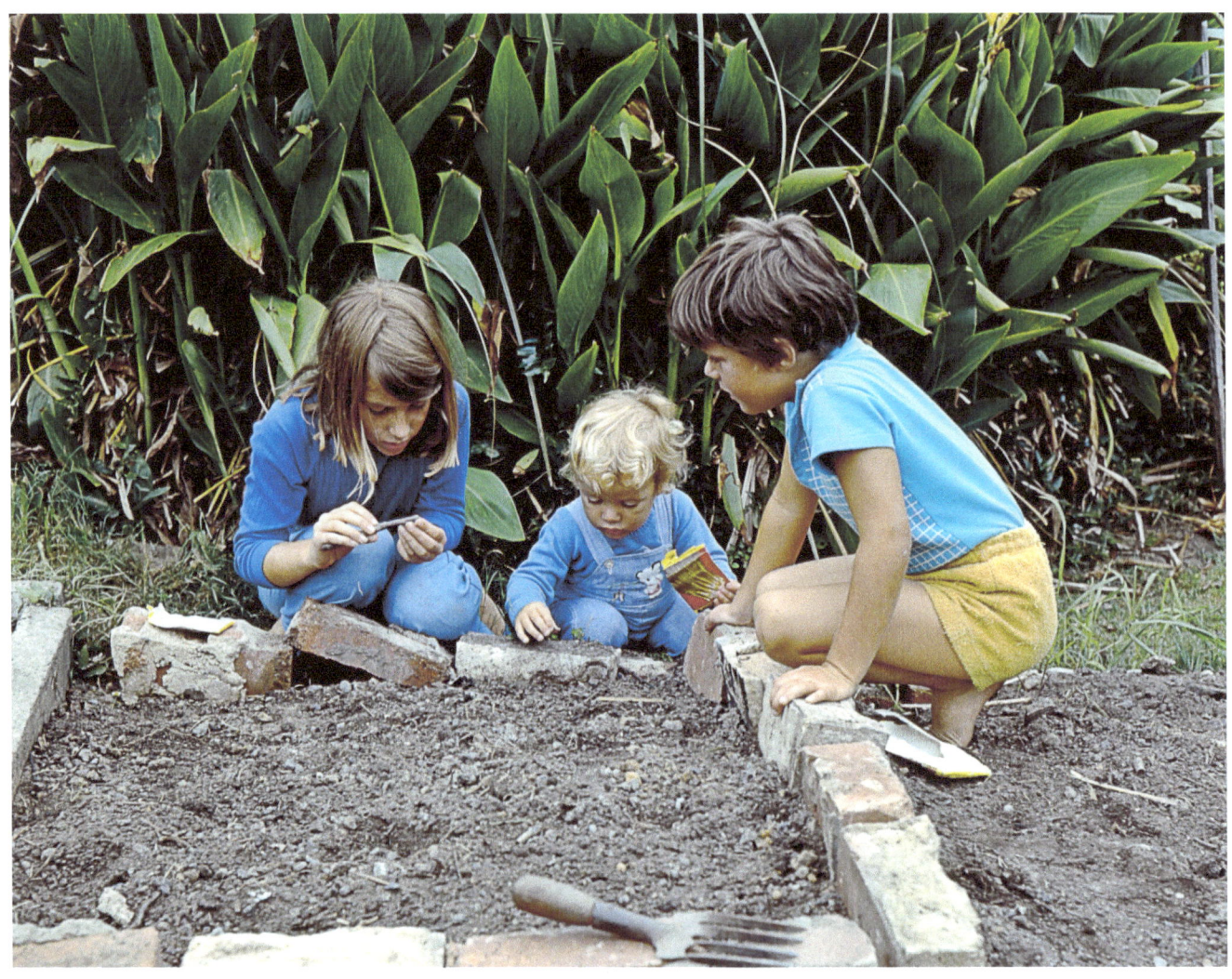

This is what I call a casual portrait. The two older children discussing something while the youngest gets on with 'planting' seeds in the vegetable garden. Obviously made under my favourite overcast sky as there are no harsh shadows.

This shot shows the benefits of having a camera handy (I was supposedly supervising the seed planting so why I had my camera with me I do not know. But, I'm glad I did!) and I'm glad that my children were so used to Dad taking pictures that they totally ignored me!

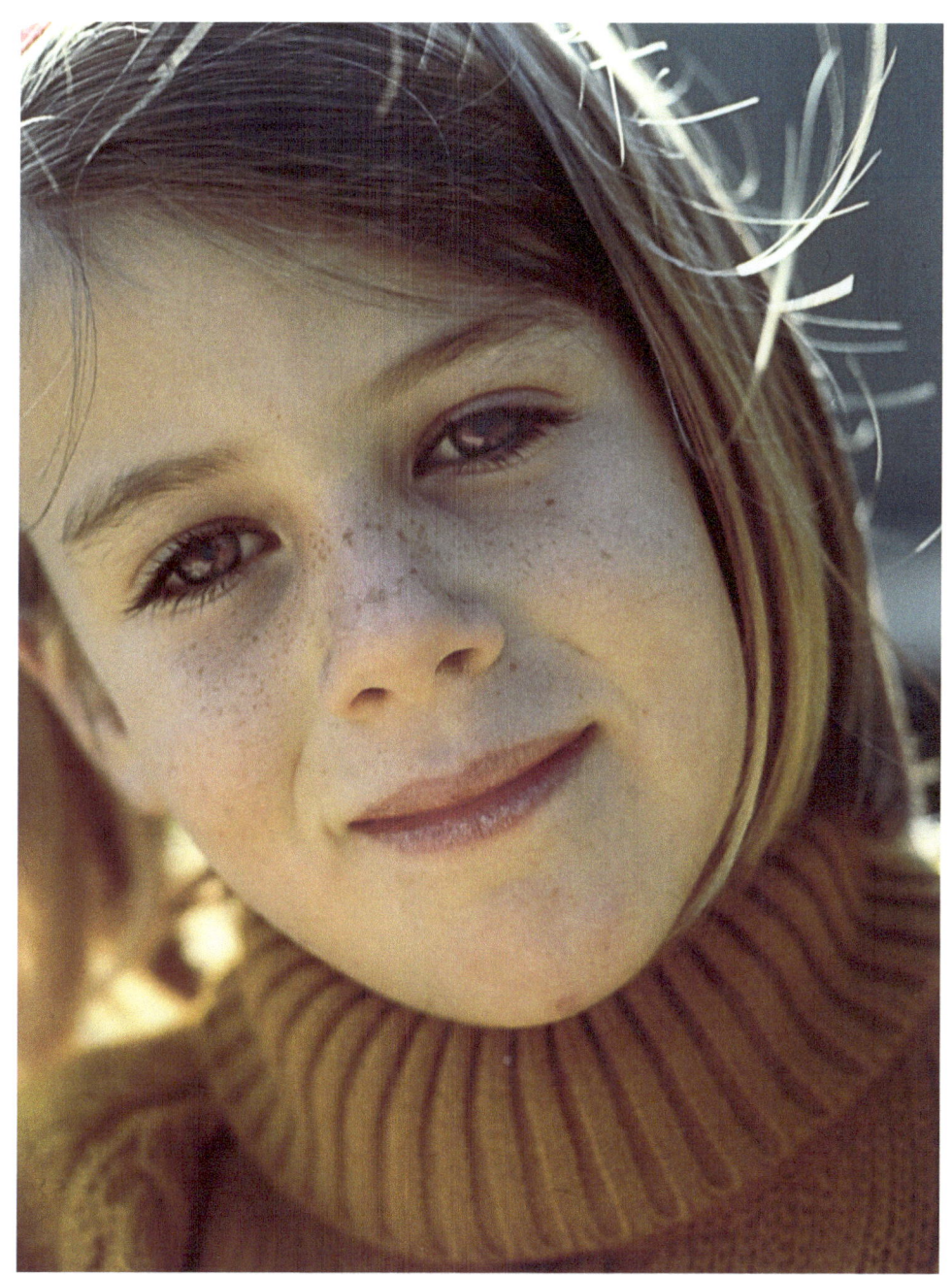

I shot this as a close up from several feet away with a lens hood as I was shooting straight into the light. I wasn't happy with the result as there was an ugly brick wall on the right so I severely cropped the picture which turned it into a lovely close up. I love the backlit strands of hair blowing on the right hand side.

Once again the meter reading was off the face and because she had her back to the sun there was no squinting or discomfort.

The sky had some clouds but it wasn't overcast so the semi shade of trees helped control the light and, fortuitously, the fallen log was in just the right position. The subject fell into just the right pose with her right arm supporting herself and giving some movement to her body. Sitting bolt upright would have destroyed this picture.

In outdoor portraiture always look for suitable props. Many people have trouble with their hands when having their picture taken. They are not too sure what looks best and as the photographer it is up to us to make appropriate suggestions. In this picture the model solved the problem herself but it is often not that easy. So keep your eyes open for anything that can be used to take care of the hand problem. Sometimes it can be something as simple as a stick that the sitter can hold.

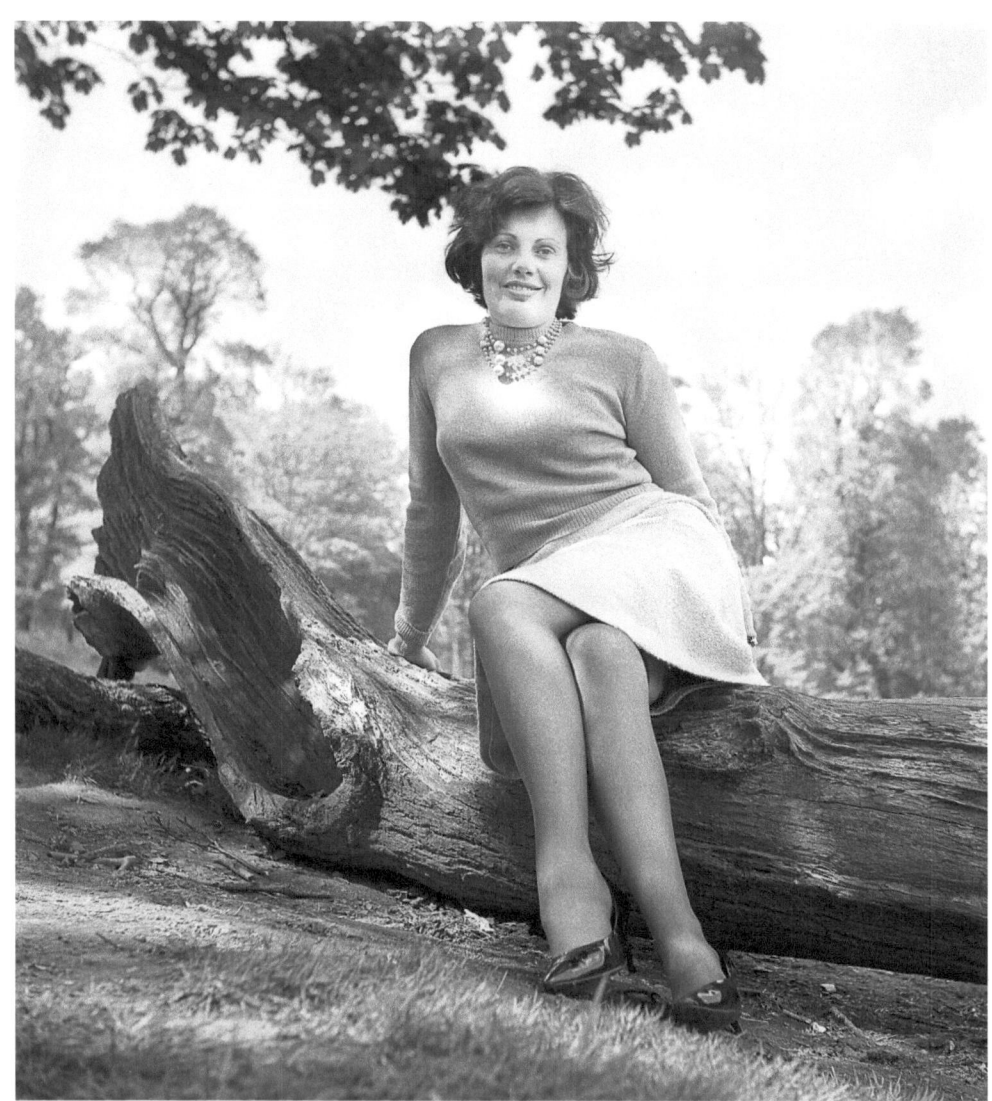

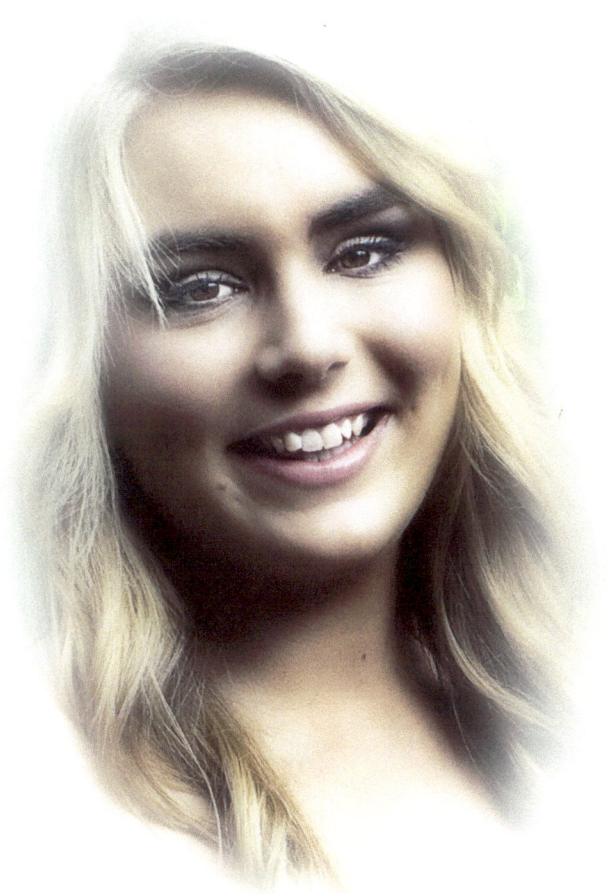

In portraiture, especially when the face is dominant, it is important that the eyes are sharp. In this picture, I have vignetted the face to get rid of distracting elements that surrounded the face. The picture was made in a garden with much foliage. In post processing I made sure the eyes and the mouth were given prominence.

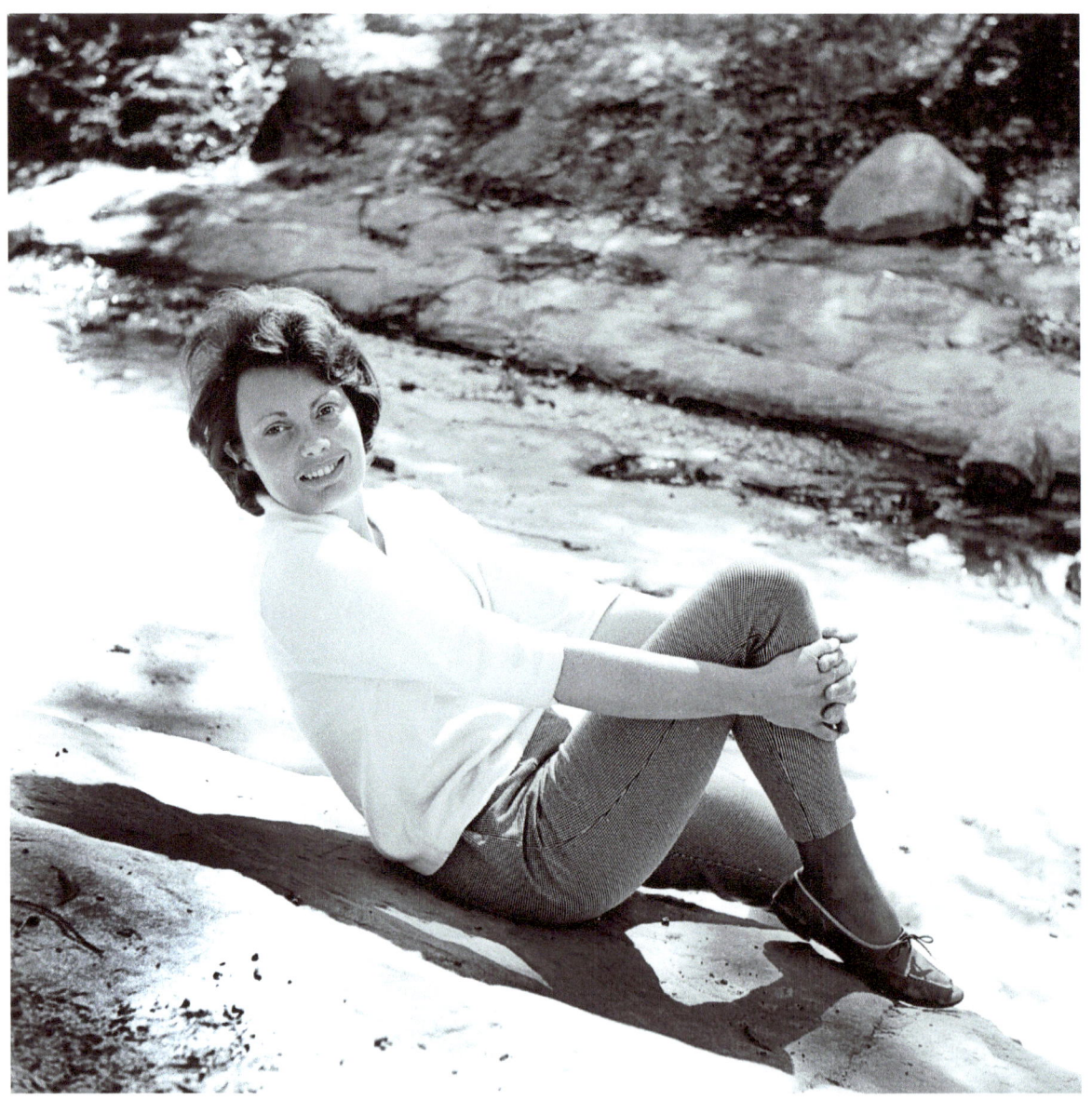

A bright sunny day but no squinting because the model has been able to turn her head towards the camera which was located so that she could do that and so avoid the bright light in her eyes. It has also allowed part of her hair to be highlighted. And the natural pose has solved the hand problem.

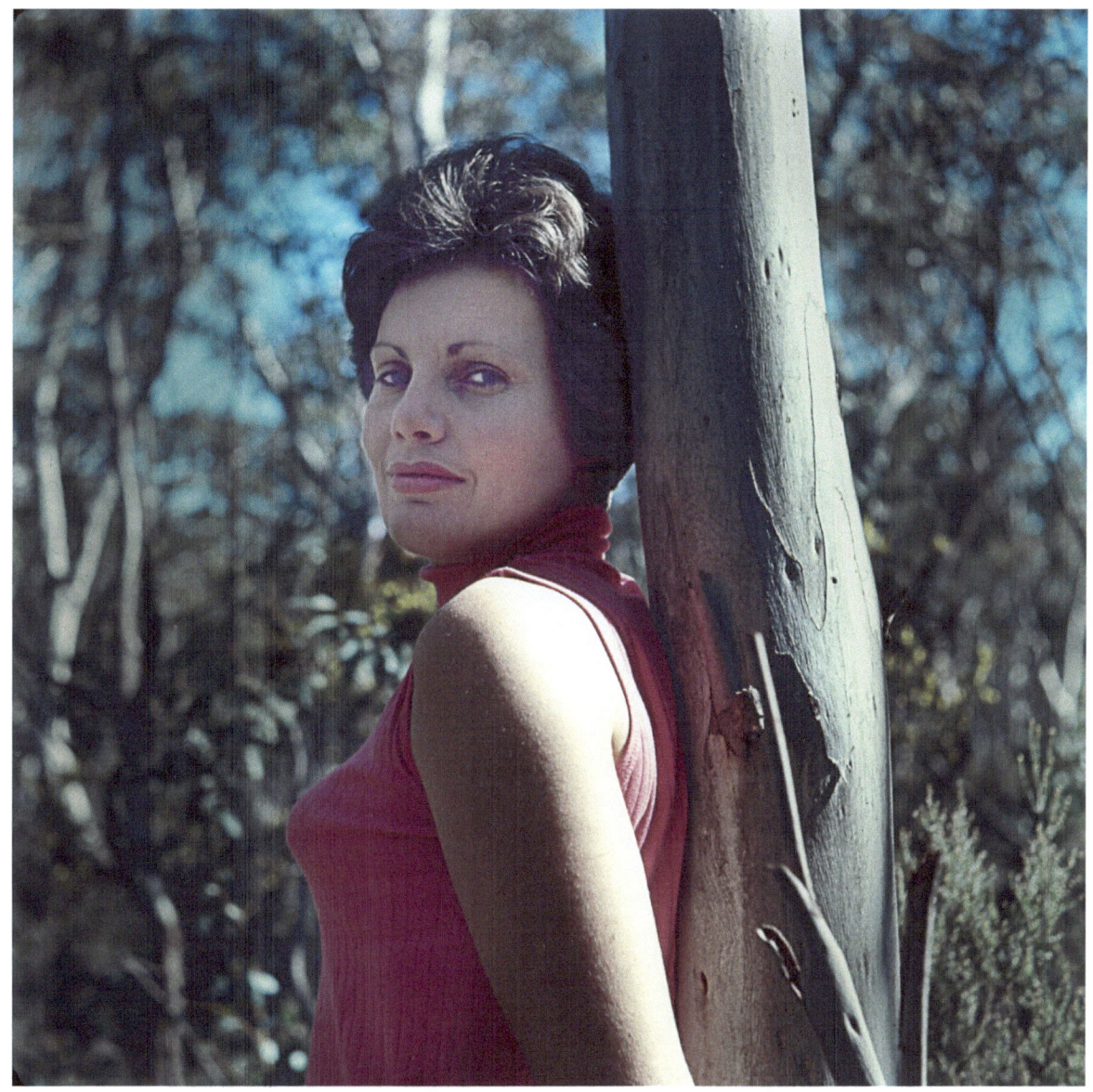

Posing the model on the shadow side of the tree has solved the squinting problem and given her something to lean comfortably against. Metering off her face has provided a correct exposure. The lit side of her arm and shoulder could have been a problem but I think it actually leads the viewer's eye to the face.

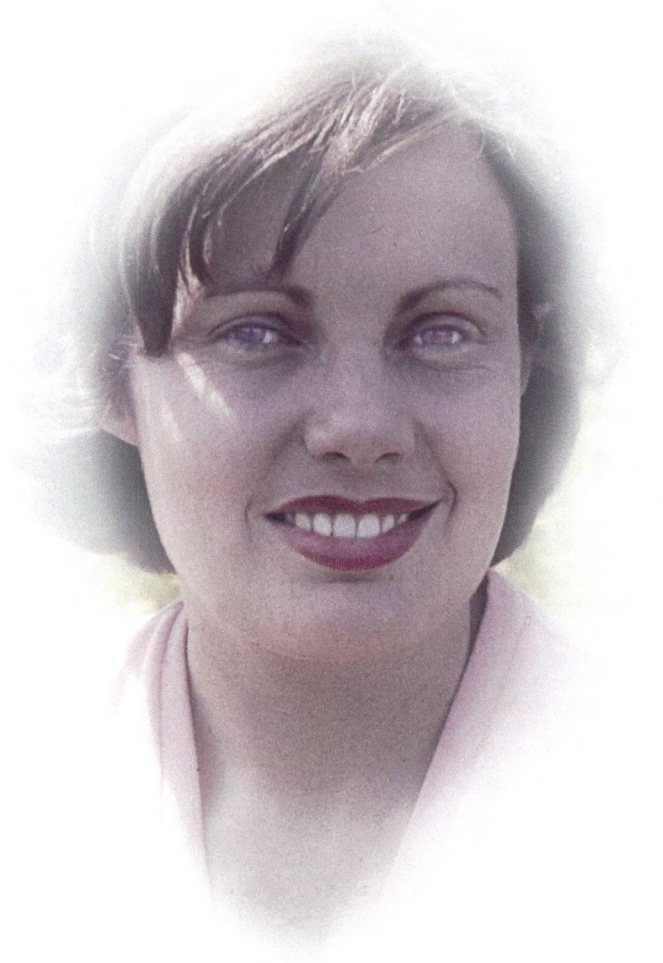

Vignetting is a useful tool in portrait photography. It allows attention to be focused entirely on the sitter's face. Ensuring the eyes and mouth are sharp is important in what is otherwise a very soft picture.

www.ingramcontent.com/pod-product-compliance
Lightning Source LLC
Chambersburg PA
CBHW051835210526
45473CB00005B/1879